THE BEAUTIFUL DANCER COLORING BOOK

BY KID KONGO

ISBN: 10: 1532863624
ISBN-13: 978-1532863622

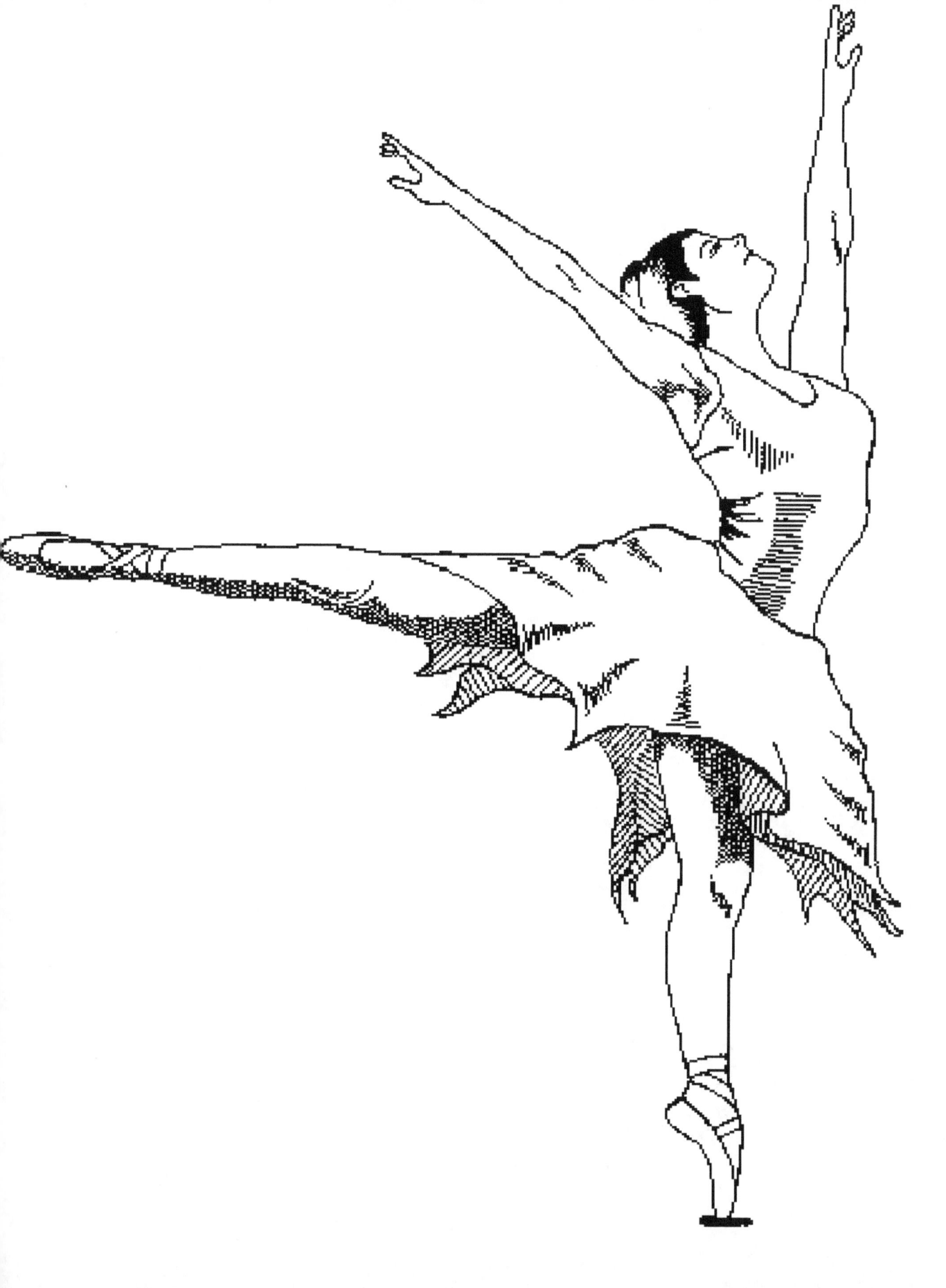

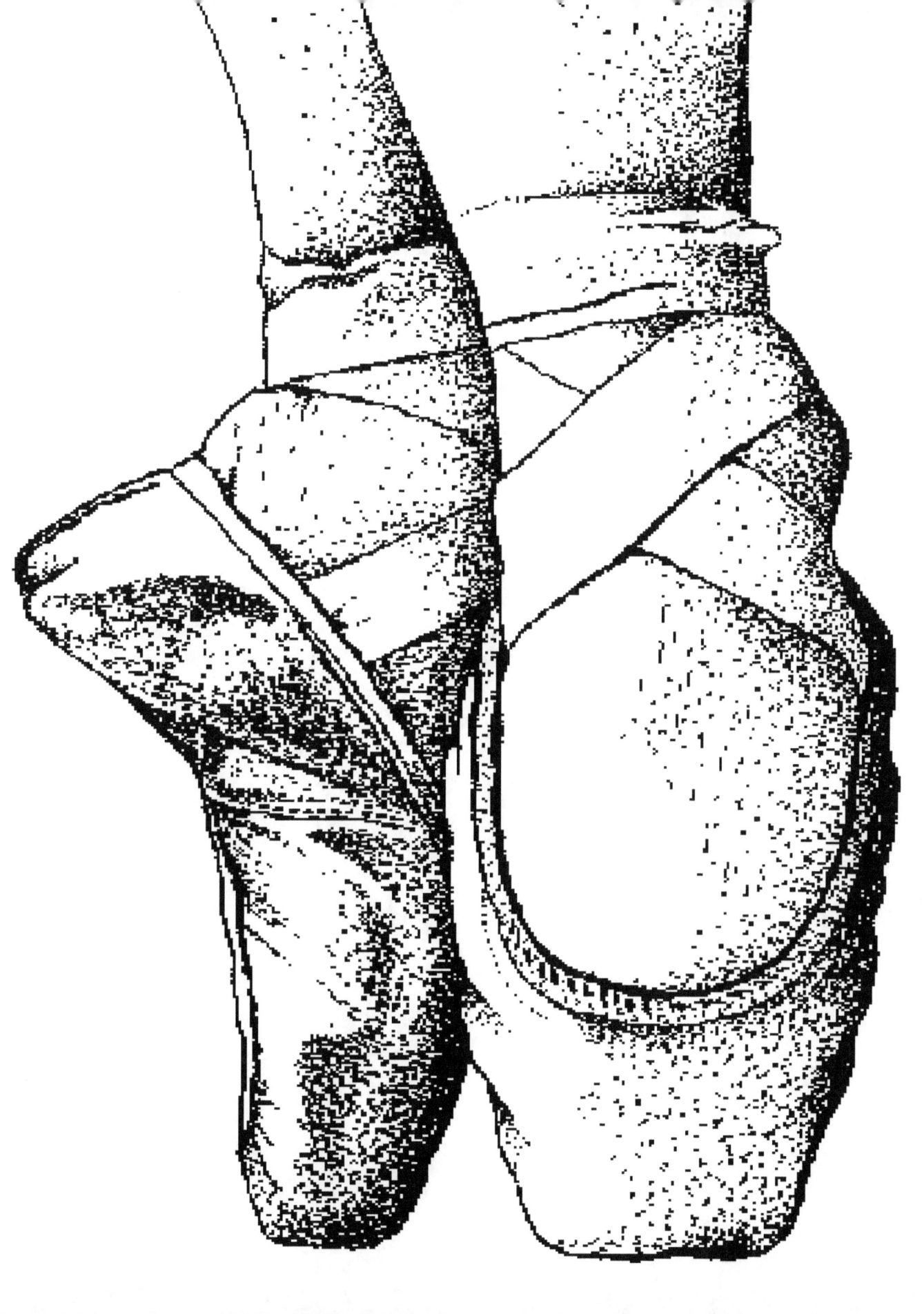

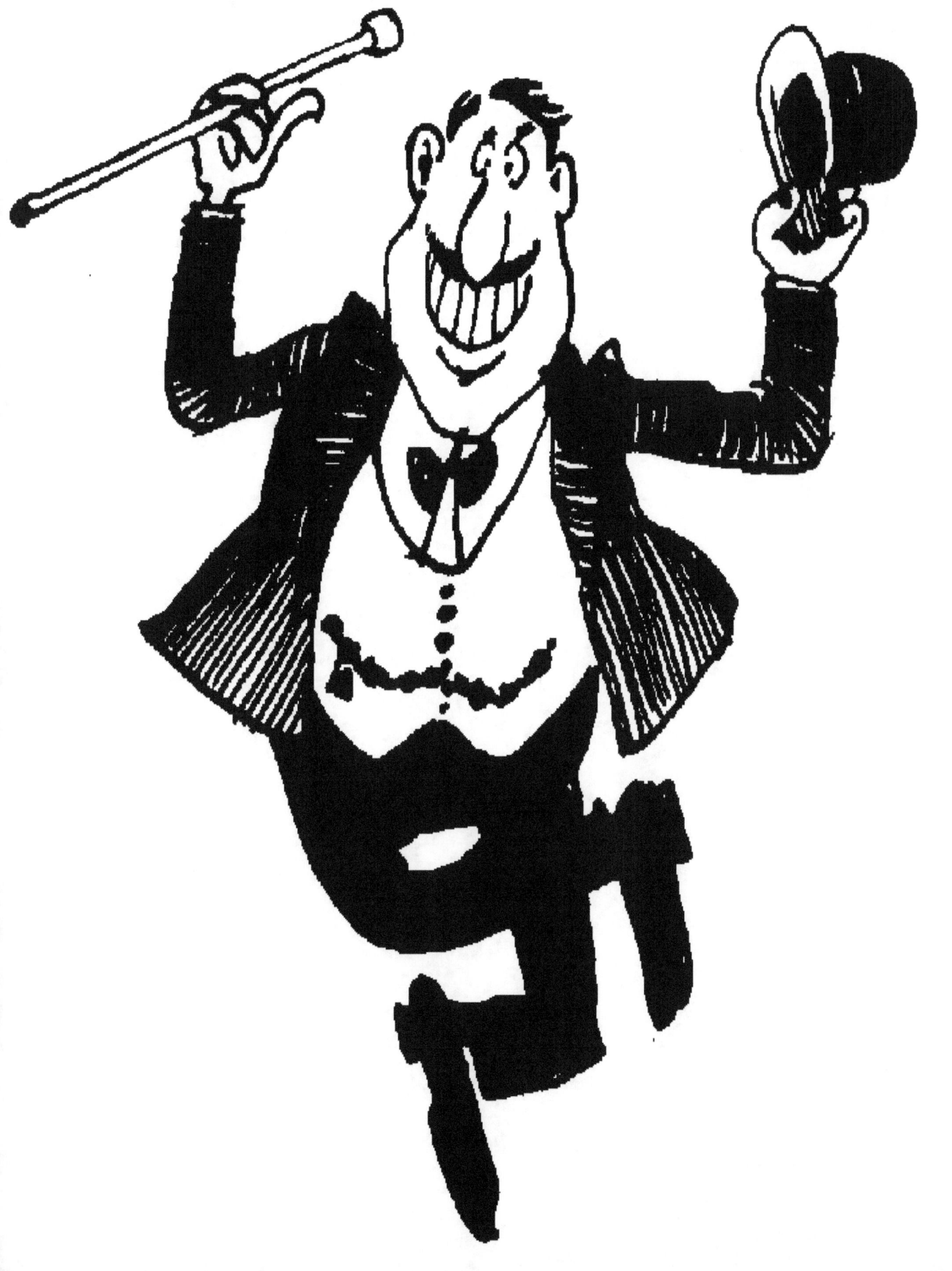

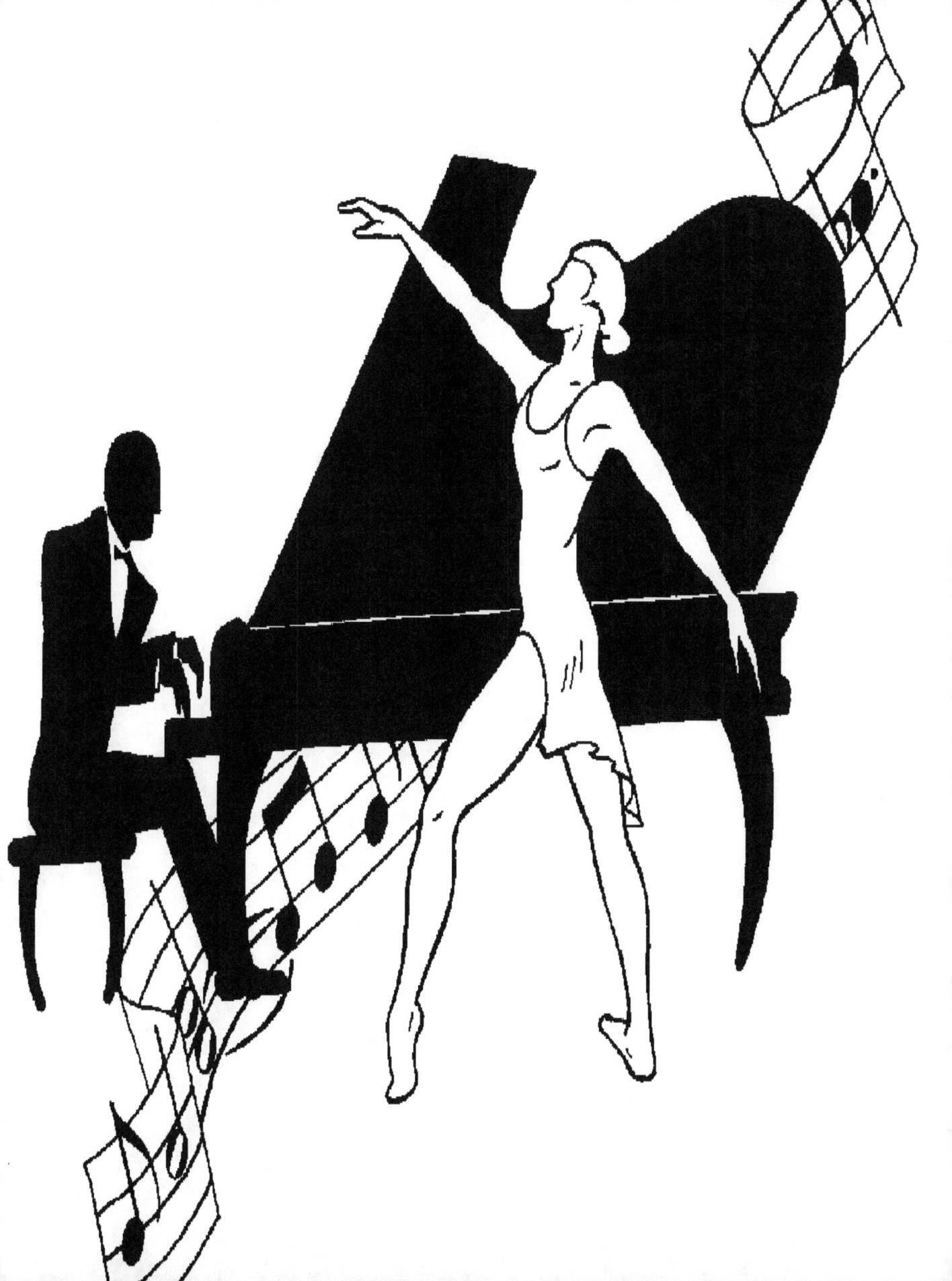

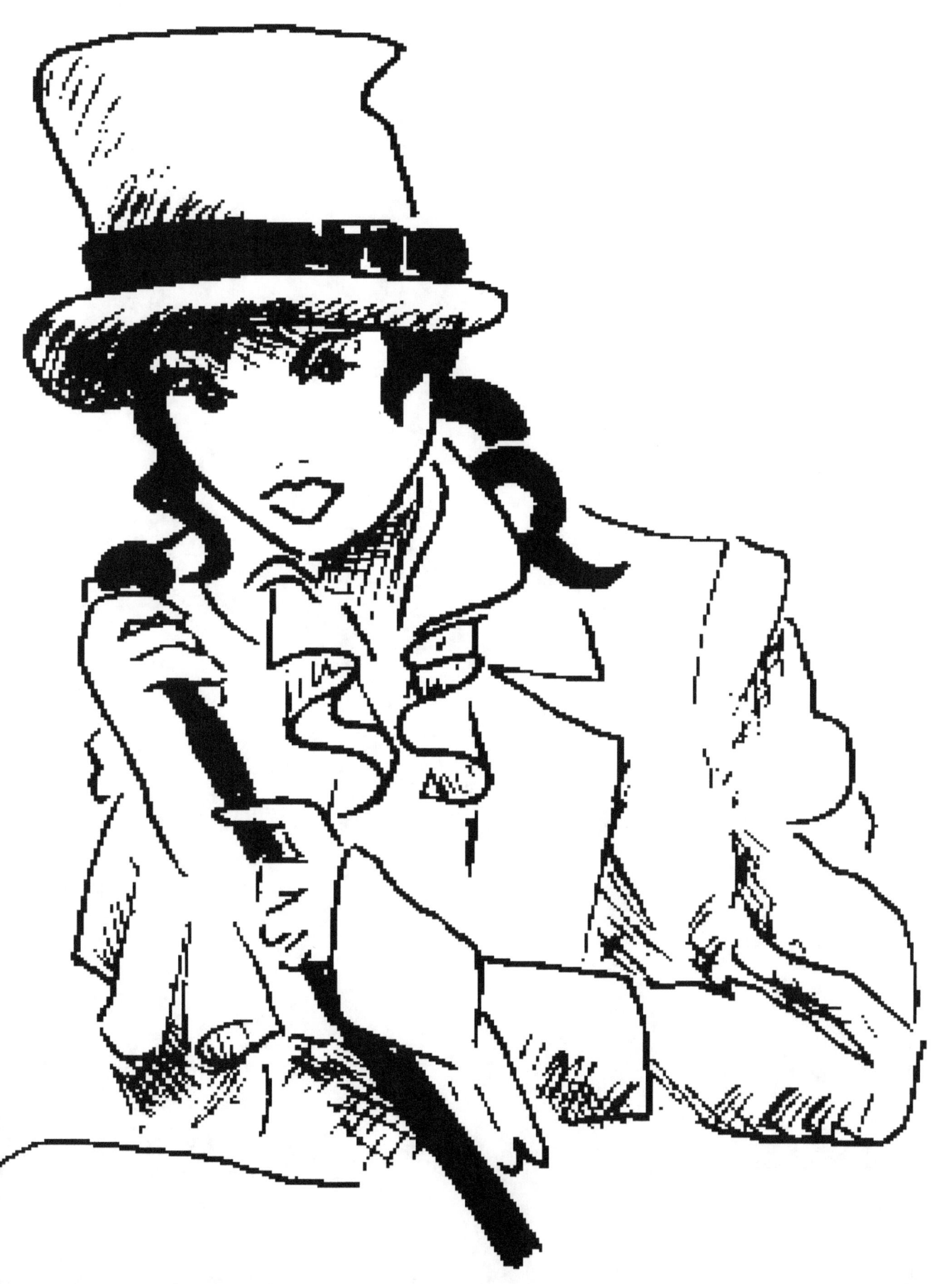

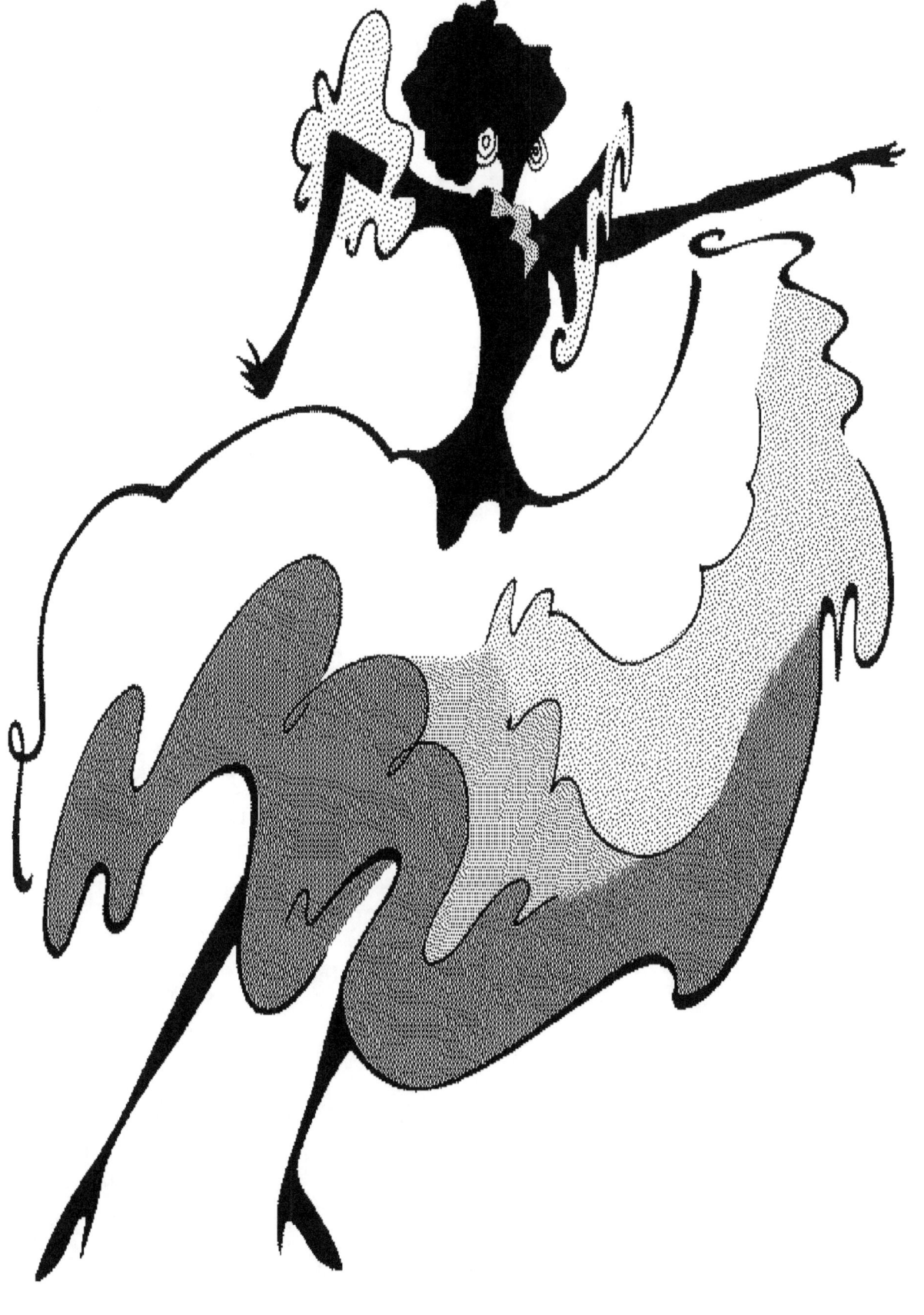

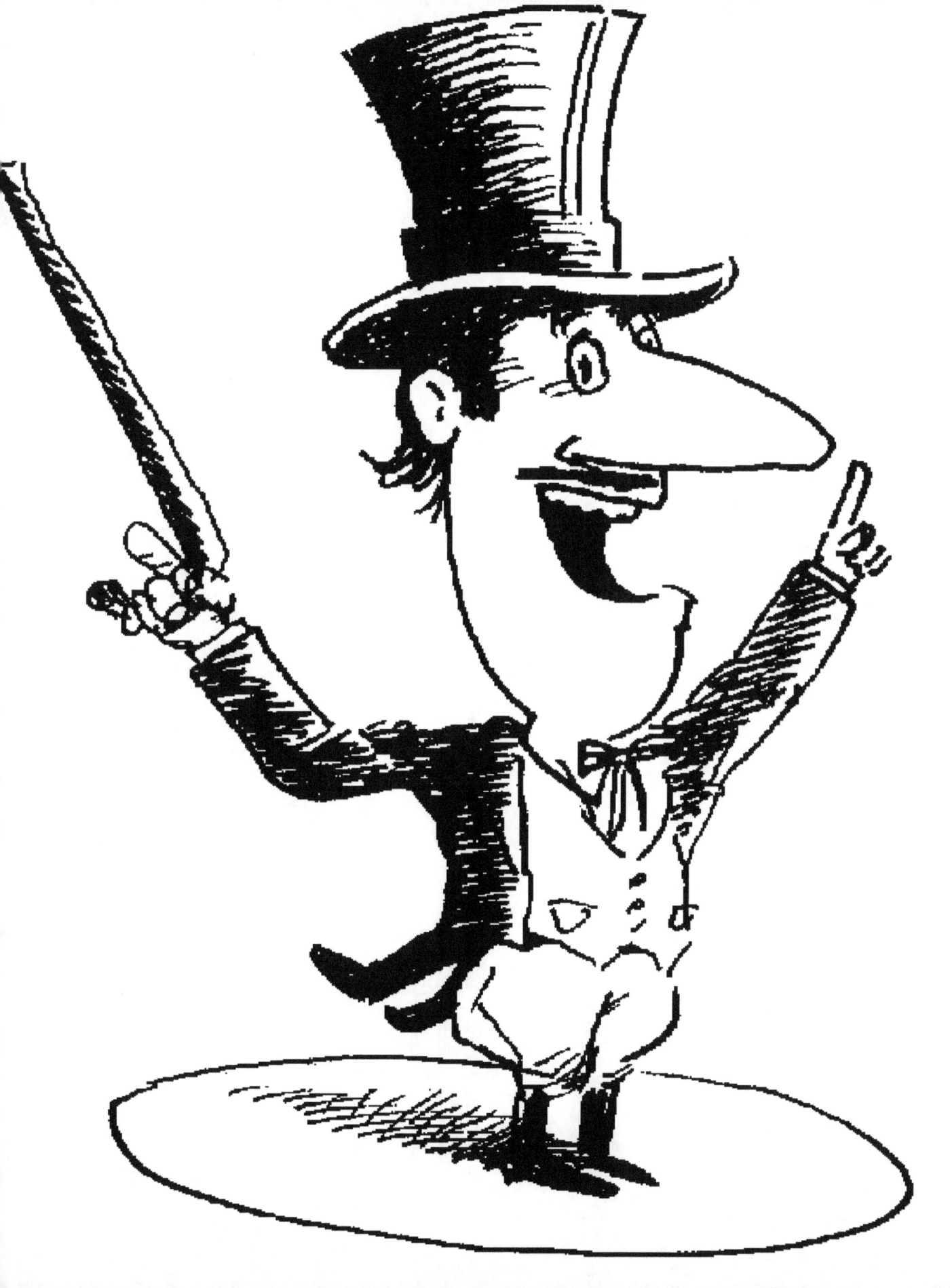

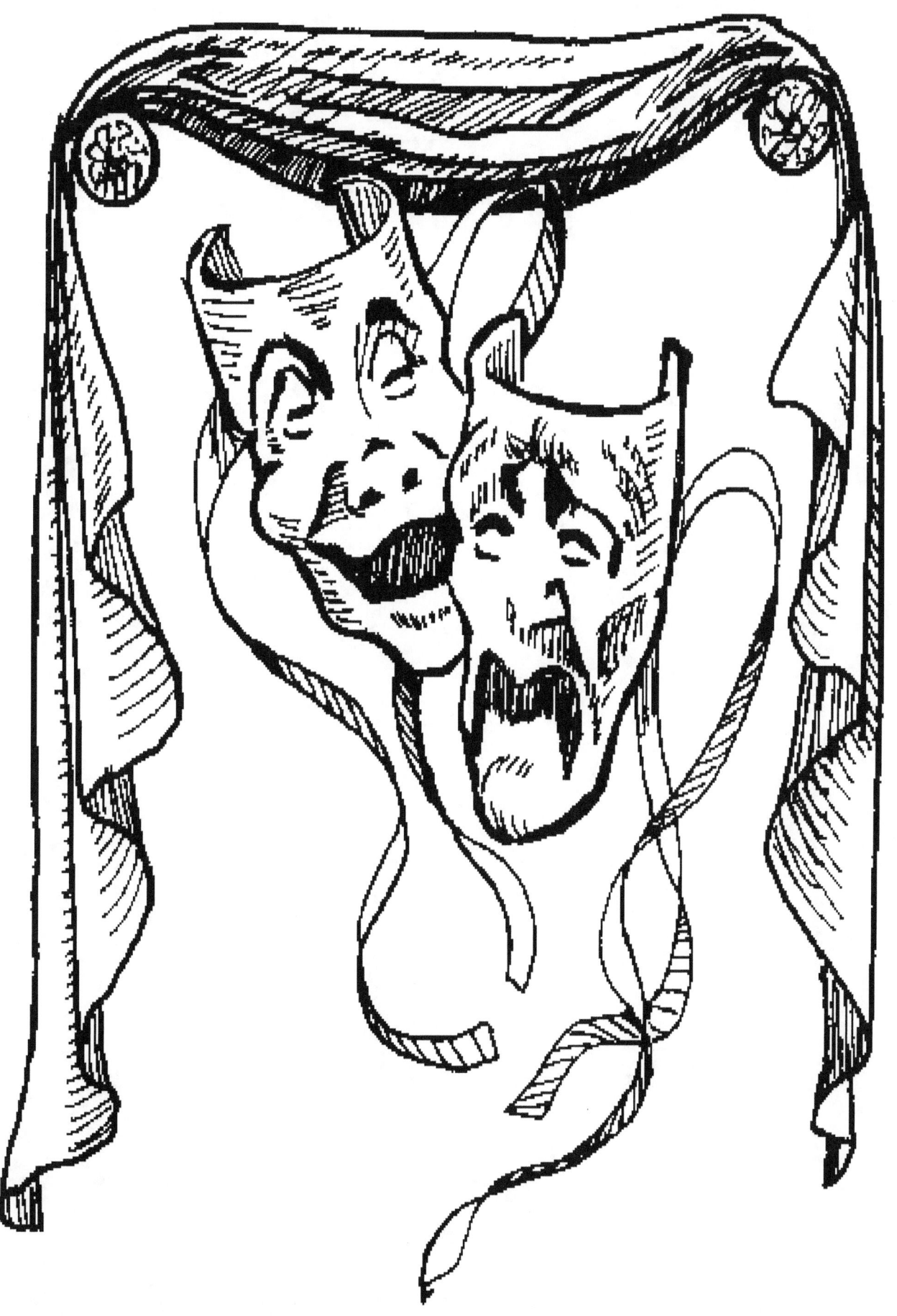

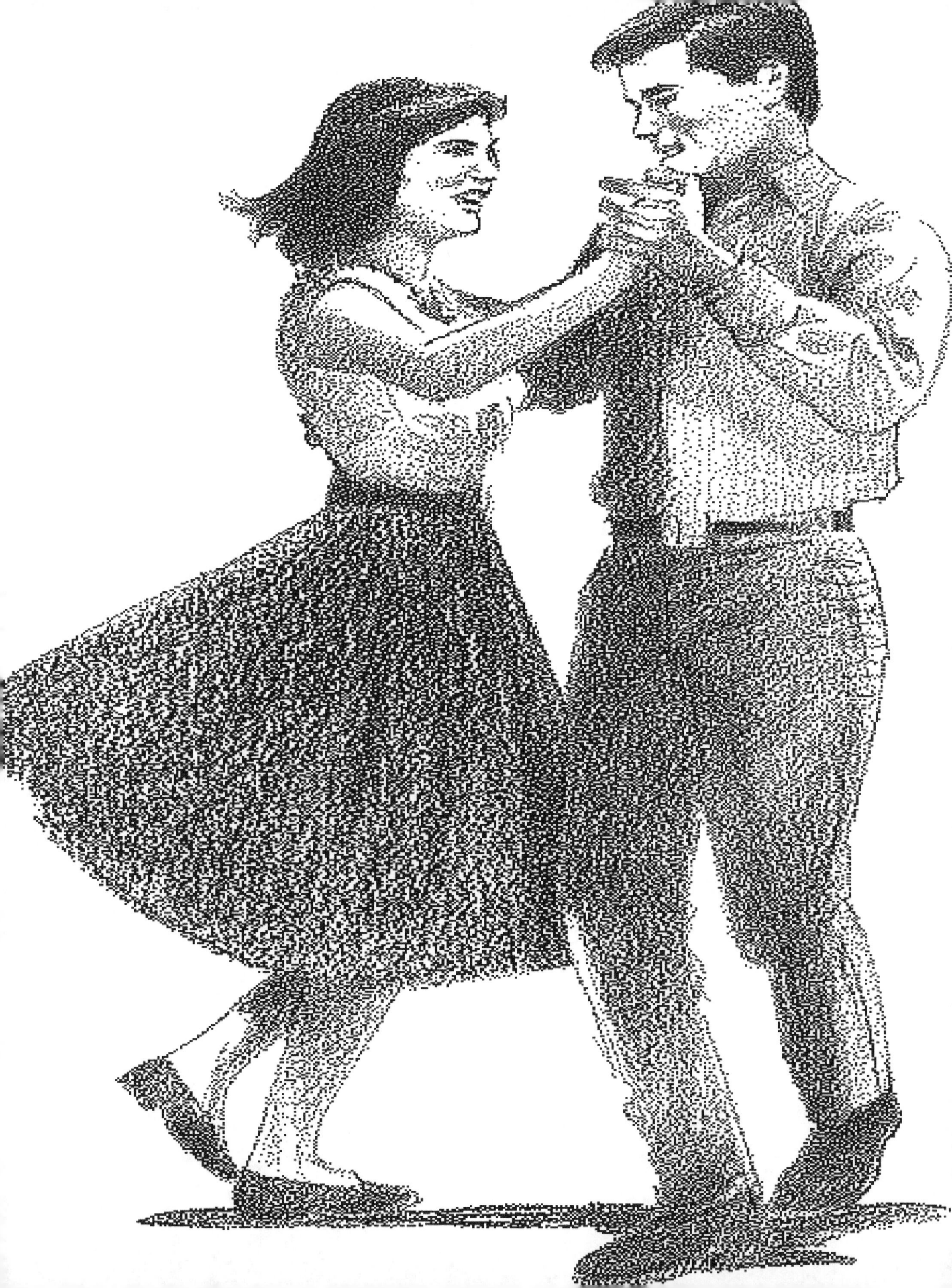

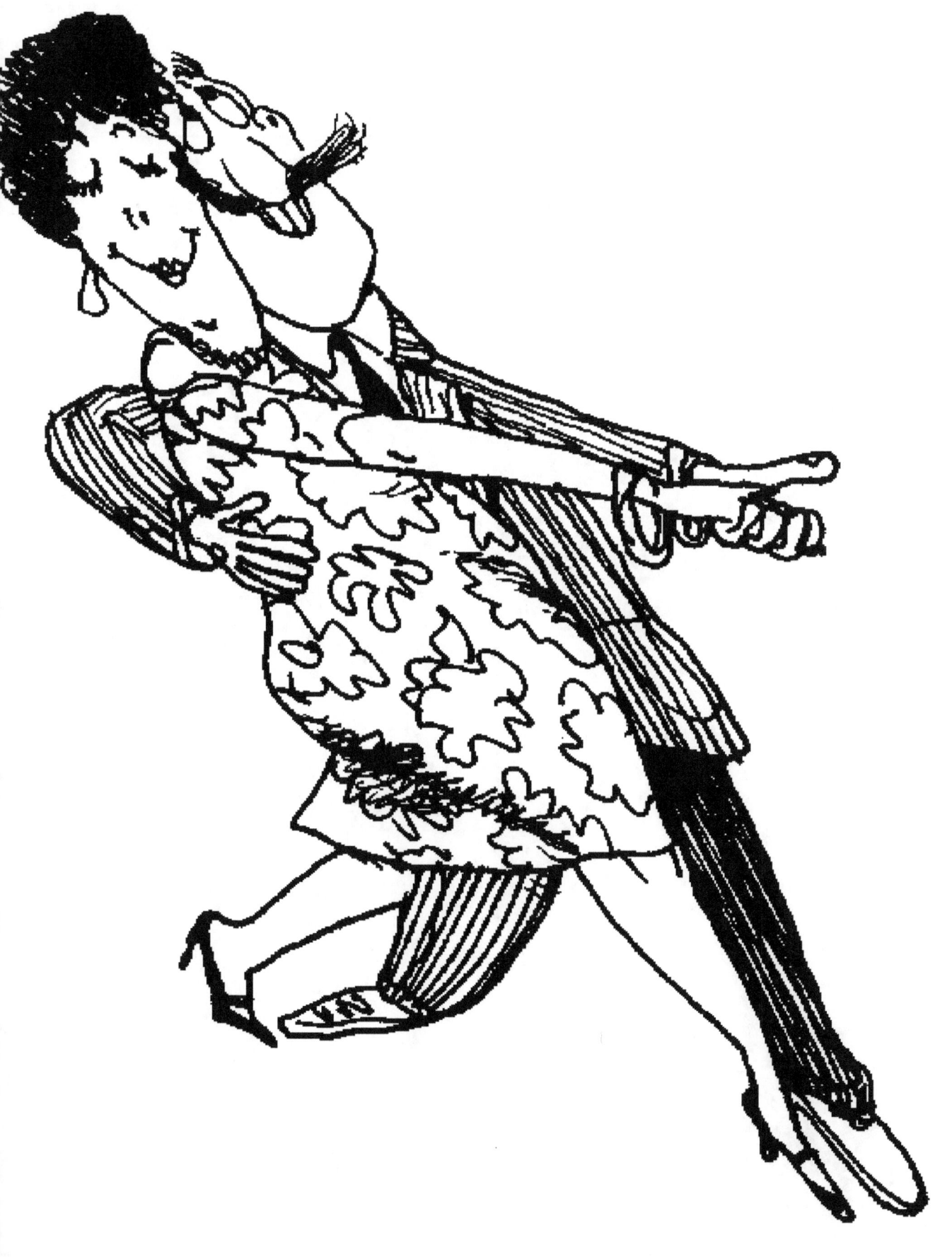

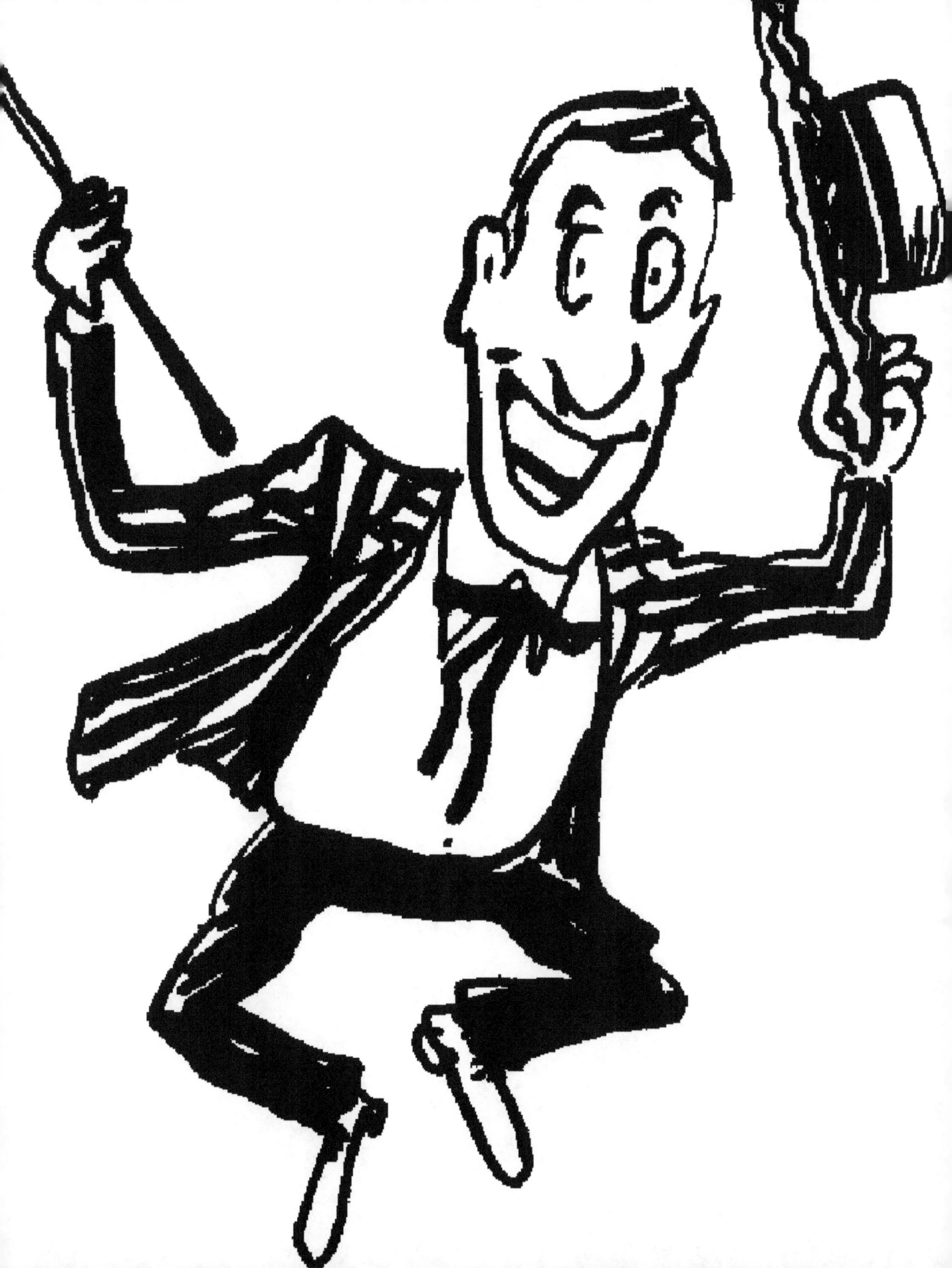

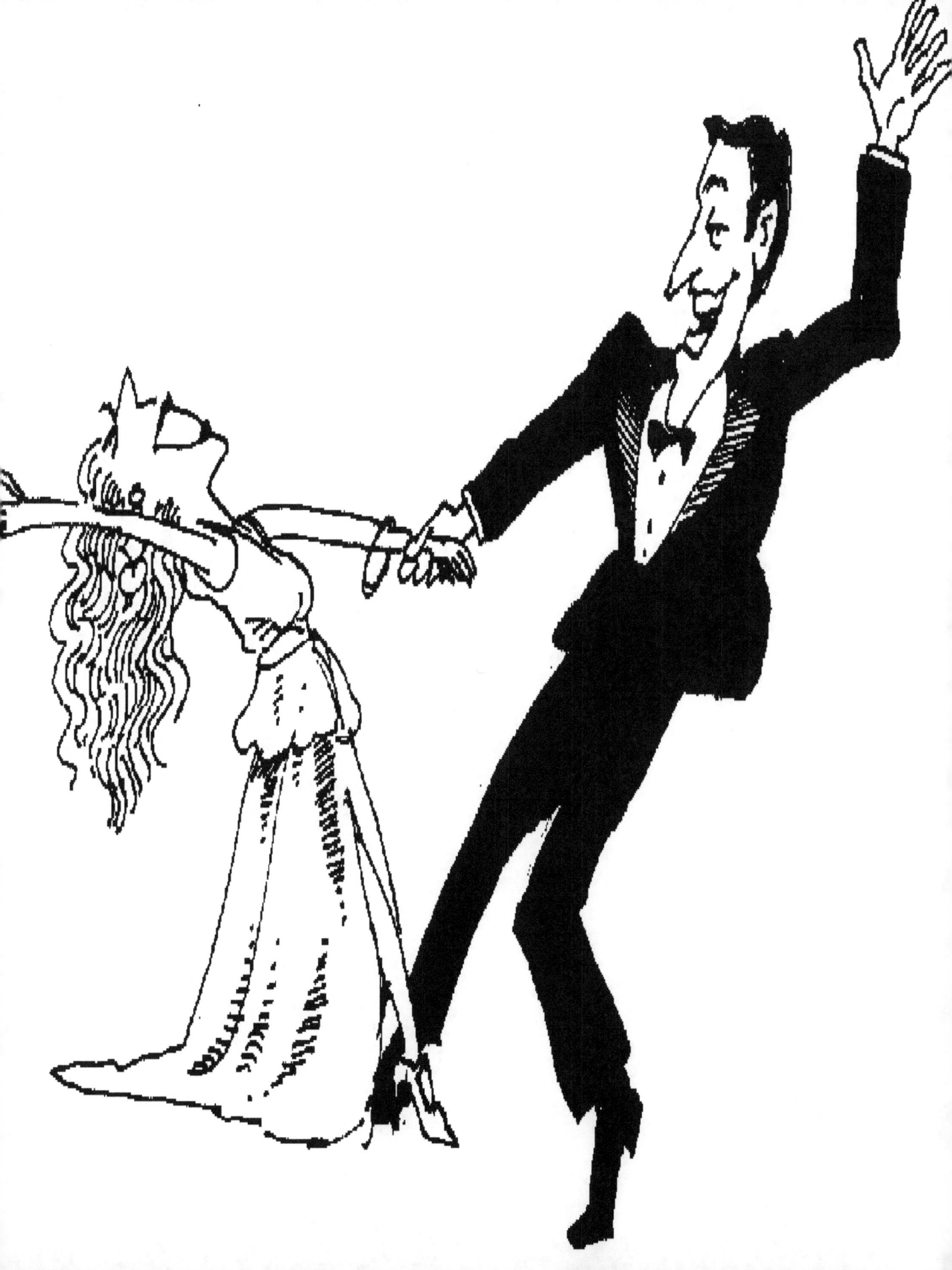

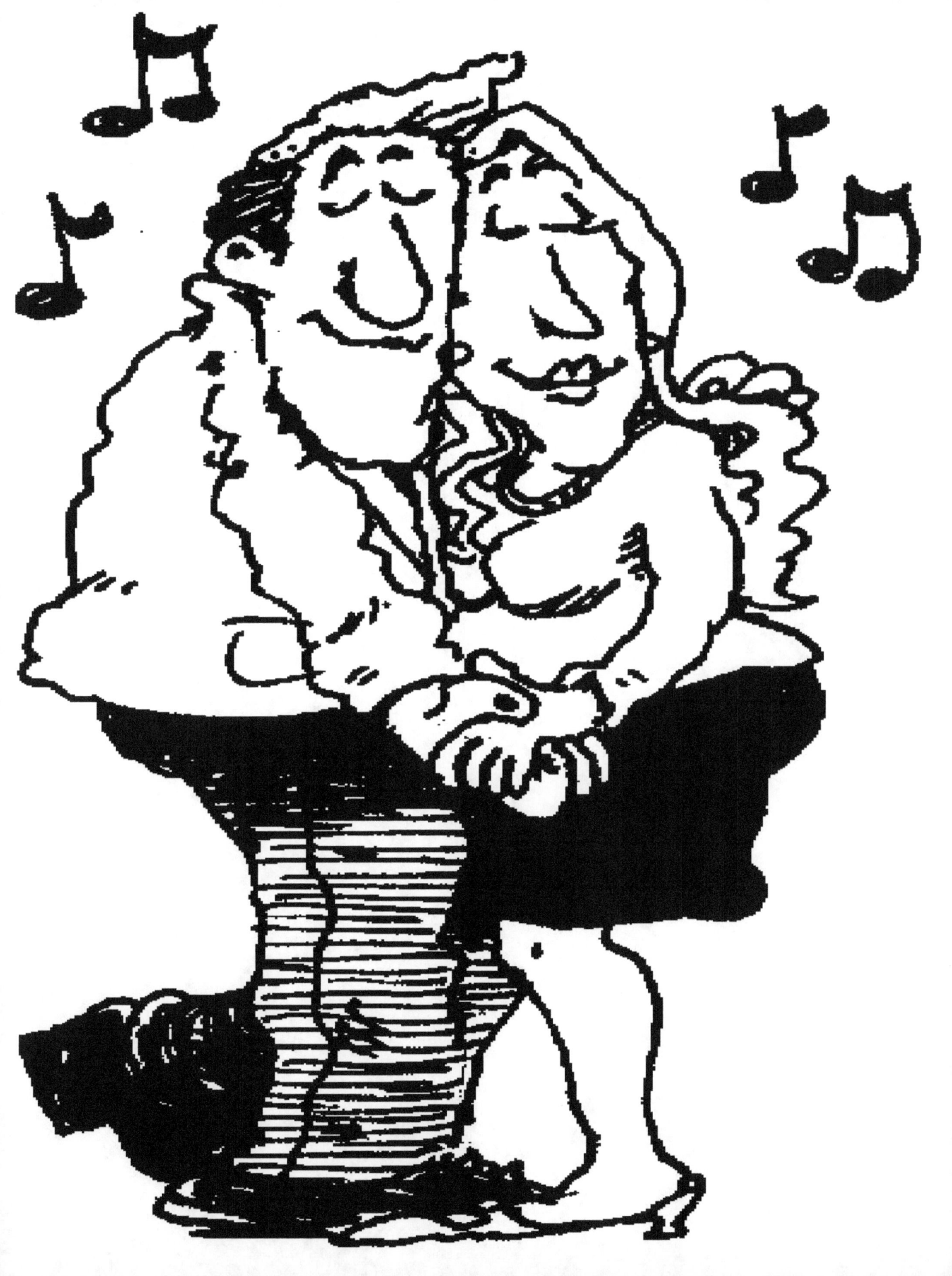

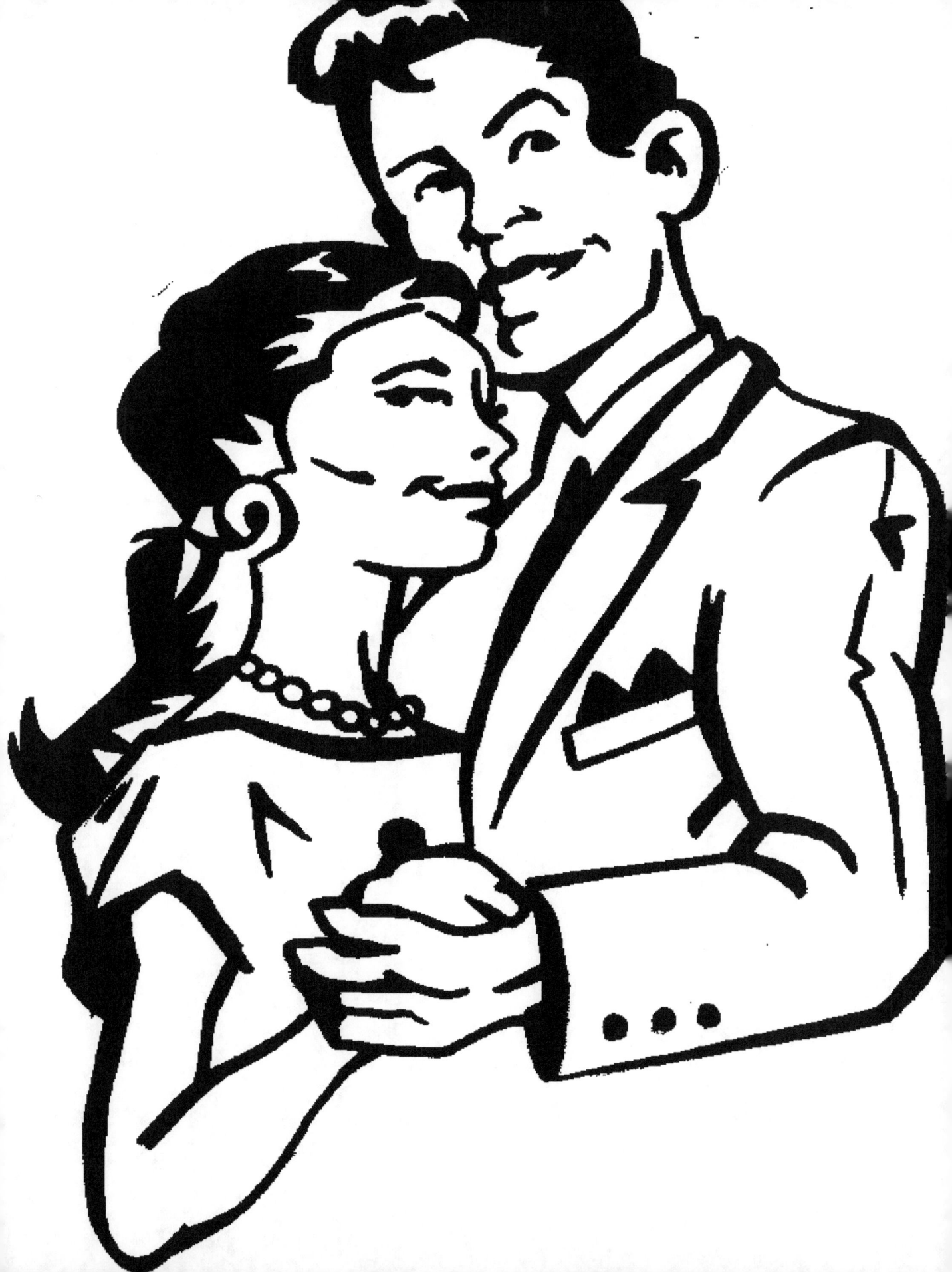

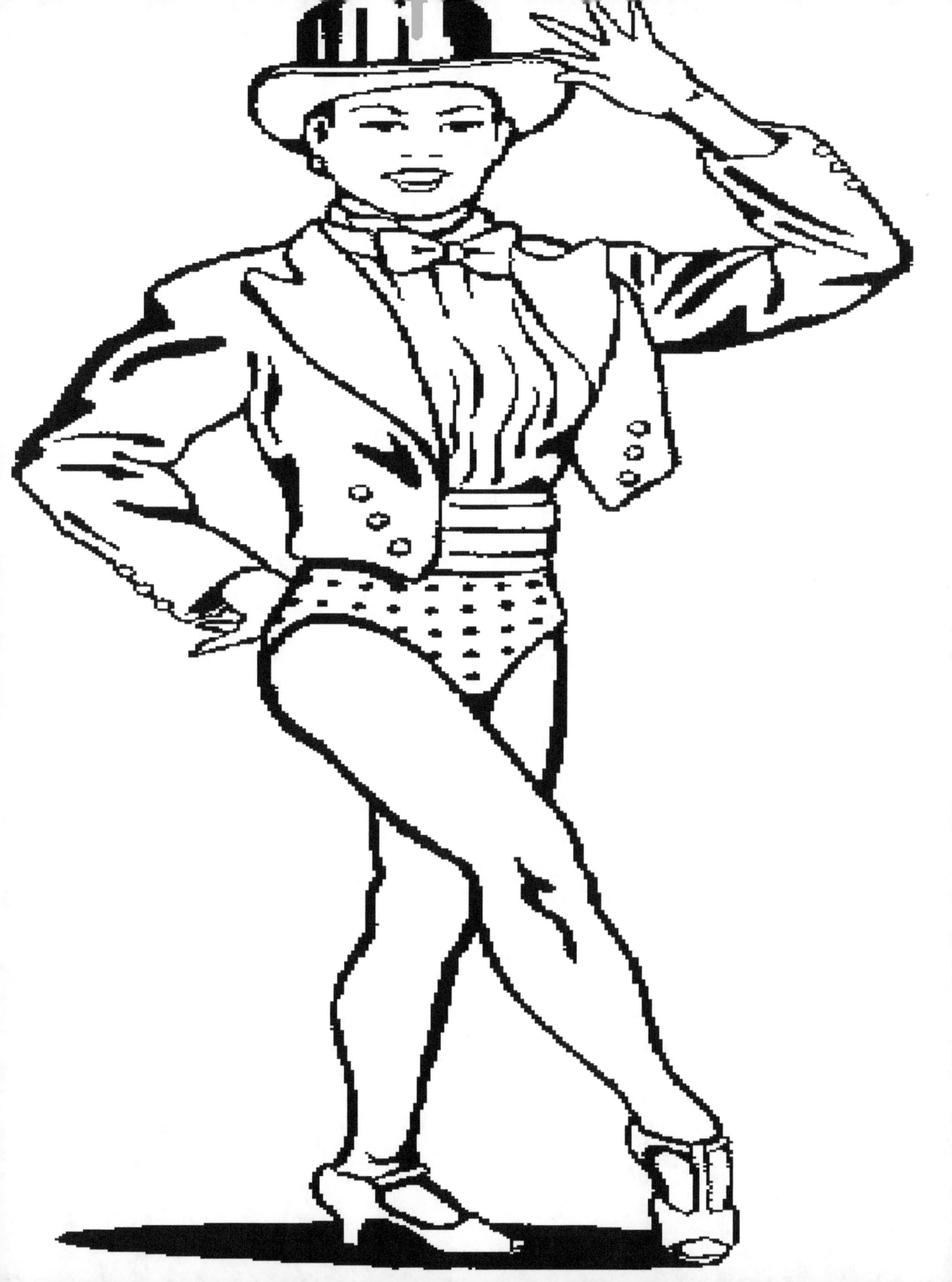

www.ingramcontent.com/pod-product-compliance
Lightning Source LLC
Chambersburg PA
CBHW080527190526
45169CB00008B/3083